Included in this volume:

SICK JOKES, GRIM CARTOONS & BLOODY MARYS
MORE SICK JOKES & GRIM CARTOONS
ILL MORE SICK JOKES & EVEN GRIMMER CARTOONS

The Complete Book of SICK JOKES

Edited by
MAX REZWIN

CITADEL PRESS
Secaucus, New Jersey

FOREWORD

"Aside from that, Mrs. Lincoln, how did you enjoy the play?"

The Complete Book of Sick Jokes is a compilation of all three of Max Rezwin's bruisingly funny collections of stories and jokes that best exemplify a particular brand of black humor. Disfigurement, mutilation and death are some of the grim subjects with which the jokes are peppered. And yet we laugh!

If a man slips on a banana peel, we guffaw. And if a gentleman in a top hat is pelted by snowballs we laugh! But if a ragged bum is pelted by the same snowballs, we feel pity—except in this collection, where the unfortunate, the lame and the maimed are equally the butts of laughter.

SICK

JOKES, *GRIM CARTOONS* &

BLOODY
MARYS

> *"Odysseus struck the hunchback on the back and shoulders with his staff. A bloody weal, raised by the golden studs on the rod, swelled up and stood out on Thersites' back. He sat down terrified, and in his pain looked round him helplessly and brushed away a tear.* The rest of the Greeks, disgruntled though they were, had a hearty laugh at his expense."
>
> THE ILIAD, *Book II*

Does the delight found in occasional sadistic laughter make you uneasy? Find comfort in the fact that this thing has been going on at least since Homer. And human beings being what they are—perverse and not altogether happy—you may safely conclude that the "sick jokes" recorded in this book will be with the human race, in one form or another, for a few more aeons.

Even a half-trained psychiatrist can tell anybody exactly why he is laughing at a "Bloody Mary" (the latest type of sick quickie)—in terms of mother fixation, or infantile aggression, or sibling hostility—but that is hardly the point. The point is that he does laugh at all at something which in the normal course of events would be considered sad. And the sadder it is, the harder we seem to laugh.

What's happening here is something much older than Sigmund Freud. Whether it's a flannel-suited adman on Madison, a movie queen on Wilshire, or just anybody on Main, the person laughing at a sick joke is reflecting as much superstition as a primitive Bushman in the middle of the Kalahari. In the most "advanced" society the world has yet known, we continue to exorcise our normal human fear of death, disease and misfortune. We verbalize the *tabu*—we joke and snicker about it.

It's Homeric laughter (in many ways), reminding man, at the dawn of the space age, that he is still the most fragile and feeble collection of living cells that ever walked the surface of this or any other earth. Yet by laughing at life, we affirm it.

Laugh hearty!

"Aside from that, Mrs. Lincoln, how did you enjoy the play?"

"And how much would you care to contribute to the Indian Relief Fund, Mrs. Custer?"

"Mommy, can I have a new dress?"
"Of course not. You know it won't fit over your iron lung."

10

"Mommy, may I go swimming?"

"You certainly may not, Sheldon. You know very well your hooks will get rusty."

"I know you're a hunchback, darling—but before you meet Mother, do try to straighten up a little."

"Aren't you the brave young man who tried to save my son from drowning when he broke through the ice?"

"Yes'm."

"Well, what did you do with his mittens?"

"Must be getting close to town—we're hitting more people."

"Mom, Dad's been hit by a car!"
"Don't make me laugh, Sheldon. You know my lips are chapped."

"Mommy, what's an Oedipus Complex?"
"Shut up and kiss me."

"Shirley, for the last time—either you stop playing with Sheldon, or I shut the coffin."

"Mrs. Lincoln, you and your damn theater parties."

12

"O.K., stranger—name your poison."

The honeymooning couple agreed it was a fine day for horseback riding. After a mile or so, the bride's mount cantered under a low tree and a branch scraped her forehead lightly.

The groom dismounted, glared at his wife's horse, and said, "That's number one."

The ride then proceeded. Another mile later, the bride's horse stumbled over a pebble and the lady suffered a slight jostling. Again, her man leapt from his saddle and strode over to the nervous animal his wife was riding. "That's two," he said.

Five miles later, the bride's horse became frightened when a rabbit crossed its path, reared up and threw the girl.

Immediately, the groom was off his horse. "That's three!" he shouted, and pulling out a pistol, he shot the horse between the eyes.

"You brute!" shrieked his bride. "Now I see the kind of man I married! You're a sadist, that's what!"

The groom turned to her coolly. "That's one," he said.

14

"Daddy, why can't I play with the other kids?"
"Shut up and deal."

"Can I play in the sand box yet, Mommy?"
"Not until we find a better place to bury Daddy."

"Mrs. Brown, can Johnny come out and play ball?"
"But you children know he has no arms or legs."
"That's O.K. We want to use him for second base."

"I don't care who you are, Fatso. Get them reindeer off my roof."

15

"Mommy, where are the marshmallows? Sheldon's on fire."

"Fellers, can I play ping pong?"
"You know your hooks won't hold the paddles."

"You get the number of the woman who hit you?"
"No, but I'd recognize that laugh anywhere."

"Mommy, one of the boys in school called me a sissy."
"What did you do, Sheldon?"
"I hit him with my purse."

16

The Indian was poised on top of a high mountain in Nevada sending smoke signals. All at once, from the testing grounds, there was a huge explosion and a mushroom cloud rose high in the air.

Mused the Indian, "Now why couldn't I have said that!"

"Now show Daddy exactly where you found that head."

"Mommy, how come Daddy's so pale?"
"Shut up and keep digging."

Sign over an electric chair:

"You can be sure. It's Westinghouse."

17

18

"Gosh, Dad—was that Ted Williams who just hit the home run?"

"What do you care, Sheldon? You're blind."

"Mommy! The power mower just cut my foot off!"

"Stay outside till it stops bleeding, dear. I just mopped."

"But Henry, that isn't our baby."

"Shut up. It's a better carriage."

"Mommy, why do I only walk in circles?"

"Shut up, or I'll nail your other foot to the floor."

"*Know any good places to eat?*"

"Can the twins come out to play?"

"No, Sheldon. You know they're both in wheelchairs since the auto accident."

"Sure we do. We just wanted to roll them downhill and make book."

"Mommy, I hate my sister's guts."

"Shut up and eat what's put in front of you."

"Watch your shooting, old chap. You almost winged my wife."

"Dreadfully sorry. Do have a shot at mine over there."

20

"Give it to me straight, Doc. How am I?"

"Well, Mr. Kipnis, your teeth are all right, but the gums will have to come out."

"Your grandma still sliding down the banisters?"

"We wound barbed wire around them."

"That stop her?"

"Nope, but it sure slows her up."

One sad little boy in Sunday School looked at a picture of the early Christian Martyrs being fed to the lions.

"Gee, look at that poor little lion in the back. He won't get *any*."

"Fred! Fred! Put down that corkscrew! I'm not really a champagne bottle—honest, Fred . ."

23

"Mommy, Mommy—Daddy just poisoned my kitty."
"Don't cry, dear. Maybe he *had* to do it."
"No he *didn't.* He promised me *I* could!"

"Doctor, I still can't see," said the little blind girl after the operation.
"April Fool!"

"Mommy, why are we having this Christmas tree in August?"
"I've told you twenty times if I told you once, Sheldon. You've got leukemia."

Then there was the model who sat on a broken bottle and cut a good figure.

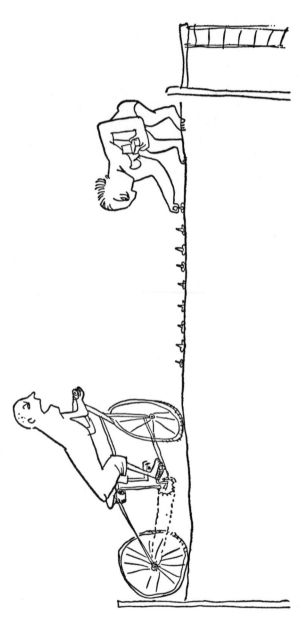

"All right, dear—I'm sorry for what I said at breakfast this morning."

25

"Yoo-hoo, Mr. Meteskey. You forgot your package."

"Mommy, am I a werewolf?"
"Shut up and comb your face."

Teacher (warning her pupils against catching cold):
"I once had a little brother seven years old. One day
he took his new sled out into the snow. He caught
pneumonia and three days later he died."
Silence for ten seconds.
Voice from the rear: "Where's his sled?"

"Can I go with you to the beach, Mommy?"

"You know your iron lung won't fit in the Volkswagen."

"Mrs. Brown, can Sheldon come out and play?"

"Now, you children know he has leprosy."

"Then can we come in and watch him rot?"

"Can I play the piano, Mommy?"

"Of course not. You know very well your hooks will scratch the keys."

"Mommy, where are the matches?"

"Why?"

"We've got to build a fire under Jimmy. He swallowed the corn before we could pop it."

"Sam," his dying partner wheezed, "I have a confession to make. *I* robbed our firm of $100,000. *I* sold the secret formula to our competitors. *I* took the letter from your desk that your wife needed to get her divorce. And Sam, *I* . . ."

"That's all right, old man. It was *me* that poisoned you."

27

28

Then there was the ghoul who sent his girl a heart for Valentine's Day—still beating.

"Now, sir. You've applied for a job as switchman. What would you do if you saw two trains approaching each other on the same track?"

"I'd throw the lever and switch one onto another track."

"And if the lever was jammed?"

"I'd turn the signals to red by hand."

"And if the signals were jammed?"

"I'd grab a red flag and run out on the track."

"And if the engineers didn't see you?"

"I'd send for my sister."

"Your *sister*? What could she do?"

"Nothing. She just loves to watch train wrecks."

29

The foreman of the lumber camp put a new workman on the circular saw. As he turned away, he heard the man say "Ouch."

"What happened?"

"Dunno," replied the man. "I just stuck out my hand like this, and—well, I'll be damned. There goes another one!"

"Daddy, get the barbecue sauce. Sheldon just fell in the fire."

"Sir, I pulled your daughter out of the water and resuscitated her."

"Then, by George, you'll marry her!"

*"Today we are privileged to have with us the head of
the recent Yale expedition to Africa."*

31

"Uncle Morris! Shirley ate a poison mushroom!"

"I'm busy, Sheldon."

"Uncle Morris! Now Shirley's fallen in the river! She's drowning!"

"The mushroom would have gotten her anyway."

Exasperated by an argument with a woman passenger as to whether she should pay five or ten cents fare, the conductor picked up her shopping bag as the bus crossed a bridge, and threw it in the river.

"You monster," cried the woman, "First you try to rob me, and now you drown my boy."

"When he said he was going to step off the top of the building onto a cloud, why didn't you stop him?"

"Man, I thought he'd make it."

"Want to lose ten pounds of ugly fat?"

"Sure."

"Cut off your head."

"Daddy, there was a man here today to see you."

"With a bill?"

"Nope. Just an ordinary nose like yours."

The cavalry had ridden to the rescue, but all the members of the wagon train were dead except the wagonmaster, who lay propped against a wheel, an Indian arrow piercing his lungs.

"Does it hurt?" asked a new recruit.

"Only when I laugh."

32

"Coach, I think they found a hole through our center."

34

There was a young lady from Spain
Who was sick as she rode on a train;
    Not once, but again,
    And again, and again,
And again, and again, and again.

There was a young girl from St. Paul
Who attended a newspaper ball.
    Her dress caught on fire
    And burnt her entire
Front page, sporting section and all.

A silly young man from Hong Kong
Had hands that were skinny and long.
    He ate rice with his fingers—
    The taste of it lingers,
But now all his fingers are gone.

"Whaddya mean, 'eeeya'?"

"Heard you were moving your piano, so I came over to help."

"Thanks. Got it upstairs already."

"Do it alone?"

"Nope. Hitched the cat to it."

"Now how could a cat pull a heavy piano like that up two flights of stairs?"

"Used a whip."

"Understand your brother fell off a scaffold and died."

"That's right."

"Frightfully sorry, old chap. What was he doing up there?"

"Getting hanged."

36

37

"Does anyone aboard this submarine know how to pray?"

"I do."

"Good. You pray. The rest of us will put on escape lungs. We're short one."

"I can hardly believe that such beautiful furs can come from such a small, sneaking beast."

"I may not ask for thanks, my dear, but the least you can do is show respect."

"How long are you in for?"

"99 years. How long are *you* in for?"

"75."

"Take the cot near the door. You'll be out first."

I LOVE LIFE AND LIFE LOVES ME

I'M AS HAPPY AS CAN BE

A HAPPIER MAN NOWHERE EXISTS....

I THINK I'LL GO AND SLASH MY WRISTS

39

A woman driver ran over a cripple crossing the street. Horrified, she stopped and called,
"Oh, dear. What can I do to help?"
"Just don't back up."

Pupil: "Me slept with Daddy last night."
Teacher: "No, *I* slept with Daddy last night."
Pupil: "Must have been after me fell asleep, Teacher."

"How can you stand it?" the young psychiatrist asked the old psychiatrist. "Day in, day out, year in, year out, listening, listening, listening!"
"Who listens?"

"What's this?" the psychiatrist asked the disturbed young man, showing him a triangle.

"A keyhole, and boy, what's going on behind there!"

"And this?" continued the doctor, showing the man a rectangle.

"A motel window, and boy, what's going on behind *there!*"

"And this," he concluded, showing him a circle.

"A porthole, and boy oh boy, what's going on behind *there!*"

"Well," said the psychiatrist, "you certainly are sexually disturbed."

"*I'm* sexually disturbed! What about you—showing me all those dirty pictures!"

40

"Peanut-butter sandwich?"

42

"What are you doing in the cellar, children?"
"Making love."
"That's nice. Don't fight."

"Do you have eczema?" the doctor asked the waitress as she kept scratching her nose.
"No special orders. Just what's on the menu."

"You made a mistake in that prescription you gave my wife. Instead of quinine you used strychnine!"
"You don't say. You owe me 20 cents more."

Mama Cannibal (to witch doctor): "I'm worried about Junior. He wants to be a vegetarian."

43

"Anything to say before I hang you?" the executioner asked the golf pro.

"How about a couple of practice swings?"

"Won't your wife hit the ceiling when you come home?"

"Hope so. Last time she put a bullet through my hat."

"How'd you get along with Dad while I was away?"

"Just fine. Every morning he took me down to the lake in a rowboat, and let me swim back."

"Isn't that a long distance for you to swim?"

"Oh, I always made it all right. Only trouble I had was getting out of the bag."

44

Willie in the cauldron fell;
See the grief on mother's brow;
Mother loved her darling well—
Willie's quite hard-boiled by now.

Little Willie with a shout,
Gouged the Baby's eyeballs out;
Stamped on them to make them pop.
Mother cried, "Now, William, stop!"

William, with a thirst for gore,
Nailed the baby to the door.
Mother said, with humor quaint:
"Careful, Will, don't mar the paint."

Introduced in 1899 by Harry Graham in a book called Ruthless Rhymes for Heartless Homes, *"Little Willie"* jingles *soon became a craze in England and America. On these two pages are a few choice examples of these* fin-de-siècle *sick jokes.*

Willie saw some dynamite,
Couldn't understand it quite;
Curiosity never pays:
It rained Willie seven days.

William, in a nice new sash,
Fell in the fire and burned to an ash.
Now, although the room grows chilly
I haven't the heart to poke poor Billy.

45

46

"That's enough out of you," said the surgeon as he sewed up his patient.

"How'd you blow that tire?"
"Ran over a milk bottle."
"Didn't you see it?"
"Damn kid had it under his coat."

"This is the third operating table you've ruined this month, Doctor. Please don't cut so deep."

"*Nice body, though. . .*"

48

"Ma'am, your husband has just been run over by a steamroller!"

"I'm in the tub. Slip him under the door."

"Daddy, is Rotterdam a bad word?"

"No, son."

"Good. My teacher has poison ivy and I hope it'll Rotterdam arm off."

"Drink your soup, dear, before it clots."

The man put his small son on the mantelpiece and told him to jump into his arms. When he jumped, his father stepped aside and the boy fell on his head.

"That will teach you a lesson," the father said. "Don't trust anybody . . . not even your father!"

"Do you miss your boy since he went away to the leper colony?"

"Oh, it's not so bad. I get some nail from him every day."

Then there was the sadistic little girl who locked the bathroom door the night of her father's beer party.

50

Each day the natives would cut the missionary's arm and suck the blood.

Finally he complained to the chief. "Kill me if you want, but I'm sick and tired of getting stuck for the drinks."

"I was a 90-pound weakling. Then at the beach one day, a 240-pound bully kicked sand in my face. So I took this course, and in two years, I weighed 240 pounds."

"Then what happened?"

"I went to the beach and a 420-pound bully kicked sand in my face."

Mother cannibal: "How many times have I told you not to speak with someone in your mouth!"

". . . And therefore, It is the decision of the head of this department that hormone experimentation on white rats shall cease immediately."

The hard-working widow instructed the undertaker to cremate her good-for-nothing husband's body.

Carefully placing the ashes in an hour-glass, she set it on the mantel, and announced: "At last, you worthless bum, you're going to work!"

"Doctor, my husband limps because his right leg is shorter than his left. What would you do in his case?"

"Probably limp."

"Are you positive I'll get well? I've heard doctors sometimes give wrong diagnoses—and treat patients for pneumonia who later die of typhoid fever."

"Don't worry. When I treat a man for pneumonia, he dies of pneumonia."

52

Two partners who could never make a success of their dress business were trying desperately to avoid their fourth bankruptcy. "I wish we were as smart as Block downstairs," said one. "He's always ready with the latest fashion. Oh well, tell you what—I'll commit suicide and you can use the insurance to start fresh."

"Fine," said the other partner, opening the window. "Out you go."

As the suicide sailed past Block's floor, he shot a glance out the window, and then called back frantically to his partner: "Cut velvet! Cut velvet!"

"These are grandma's ashes."
"Oh, did the poor old lady pass away?"
"No. Just too damn lazy to get an ashtray."

53

54

"I was plodding through the woods when suddenly a giant brown bear grabbed me from behind and made me drop my gun. He picked it up and stuck it in my back."

"What did you do?"

"What *could* I do? I married his daughter."

"Mommy, can I brush my teeth?"

"All right. Get the jar."

Then there was the man who died from drinking varnish. It was an awful sight, but a beautiful finish.

MY TEACHER IS SO VERY NICE,
I ALWAYS TAKE HER GOOD ADVICE;
SHE'S JUST AS SOFT AS BUNNY FUR—
...I THINK I'D LIKE TO SLEEP WITH HER...

"Pilot to tower. Out of gas three hundred miles over Atlantic. What shall I do?"

"Tower to pilot. Repeat after me. Our Father who art in heaven . . ."

"Doctor, what can I do about these little green men crawling all over me?"

"Just don't brush any on me."

"Taxidermist, I would like you to do something with these two dead pet rabbits of mine."

"Would you like them mounted, Madam?"

"No. Just holding hands."

56

57

"You've helped me a hell of a lot," the patient told the analyst as he pointed the gun. "But now you know too much."

"Doctor, come quickly. My husband has swallowed a fountain pen."

"I'll be right over. What are you doing in the meantime?"

"Using a pencil."

"Now that my analysis is over, what kind of a husband would you advise me to get, Doctor?"

"Just get a single man. Leave the husbands alone."

58

"Mommy, when can I have some soda?"
"Shut up and drink your beer."

"Must I eat this whole egg, Mommy?"
"Damn right."
"Beak and all?"

As Fritz pushed their mother over a cliff, he said:
"Look, Hans. No Ma."

Message in a fortune cookie: "See your doctor. You
now have Asiatic Flu."

59

"Don't you just wish you were a barefoot boy again?"

"Not me. I used to work on a turkey farm."

"Understand you buried your wife last week."

"Had to. Dead, you know."

Then there was the neat nurse, who made the patient without disturbing the bed.

Then there was the pregnant bedbug that had a baby in the spring.

"If you fall off that rock and break your leg, don't come running to me."

"Doctor, Doctor! Come quickly! My husband has swallowed a mouse."

"Wave a piece of cheese in front of his mouth. I'll be right over."

(*The curtain is lowered for fifteen minutes to denote the passage of a quarter of an hour.*)

"Why you stupid woman! Why are you waving a herring in front of his mouth?"

"Now I've got to get the cat out, first."

Then there was the lucky man who had a wife and a cigarette lighter—and they both worked.

61

62

Then there were the three bears. One married a giraffe. The other two put him up to it.

"Oh, Mrs. Brown, is your son Sheldon spoiled!"
"My Shelley spoiled! How can you say such a thing?"
"Well, if you don't believe me, come down in the street and see what the garbage truck just did to him."

"I can't play archery any more."
"Lose your arrows?"
"Nope. All stuck in Mommy."

Sign in a funeral parlor window:

"We give Green Stamps."

ACKNOWLEDGMENT is made to the following publications for cartoons used in this book:
University of Illinois CHAFF (*Cover illustrations and pages 38, 35*)

The Yale RECORD (*Page 30*)
Purdue University RIVET (*Page 11*)
University of Illinois SHAFT (*Pages 19, 24, 33, 35, 47, 60*)
University of Missouri SHOWME (*Pages 13, 22, 41, 51*)

MORE

SICK JOKES

&

GRIMMER CARTOONS

MORE
SICK JOKES
& *GRIMMER*
CARTOONS

ACKNOWLEDGMENTS

The editor wishes to thank the following for cartoons used in this book:

University of Illinois CHAFF *(Pages 22, 30, 47, and cover drawings)*

Stanford CHAPARRAL *(Pages 33, 59)*

Arizona KITTY KAT *(Page 19)*

Bradley LEER *(Page 42)*

Sewanee MOUNTAIN GOAT *(Page 58)*

6

MORE

SICK JOKES

&

GRIMMER CARTOONS

"Broke my kid of biting his nails."
"Really? How?"
"Knocked his teeth out."

"But, Mother, none of the other fellas have to wear high-heeled shoes."
"Shut up, for heaven's sake, we're almost at the Draft Board."

"I was abroad myself for two years, but a psychiatrist fixed me up."

10

The Lone Ranger and Tonto found themselves suddenly surrounded by 500 screaming Indians ready to attack.

"Tonto," the masked man said, "looks like we're in trouble."

His companion turned to him and said, "What do you mean *we*, paleface?"

A young reporter, told to cut down the size of his news stories, wrote his next as follows:

"Rodney Fenster looked up the shaft at the Royal Hotel this morning to see if the elevator was on its way down. It was. Age 25."

"I don't care what star you're following. Get your camel out of my sandbox!"

The latest in drinks: Vodka and milk of magnesia. It's called a Phillips Screwdriver.

"Hang loose, Fred."

A Scotchman had been keeping a vigil at the bedside of his dying wife for several days. One evening he said, "Agnes, I must go out on business, but I will hurry back. Should you feel yourself slipping away while I'm gone, please blow out the candle."

"Can Sheldon come out and play?"
"You know he caught pneumonia three days ago and died."
"Can we use his sled?"

"George, why must you go on torturing me?"

13

"Got a cigarette?"

"Here. Take the pack."

"Thanks. Got a match?"

"You can keep this lighter."

"Thanks again. Say, have you got an oil well or something?"

"No. Lung cancer."

The veteran battleship was in port on exhibition to the public; on its deck was an inscribed bronze plaque. "And here," said the guide solemnly, "is where our gallant admiral fell."

A spry little old lady piped up: "Well, no wonder! I nearly tripped on the damn thing myself."

His wife lay on her deathbed.

"John," she pleaded, "I want you to promise me that you'll ride in the same car with mother at my funeral."

"Okay," sighed the husband, "but it's going to ruin my whole day."

"Mrs. Finster, can Sheldon come to our party?"

"Of course not. You know he had an accident and broke both his legs."

"Yeah, we know. But we wanna crack our walnuts between his casts."

Coroner: "What were your husband's last words?"
New Widow: "He said, 'I don't see how they make a profit on this stuff at a dollar and a quarter a fifth.' "

An American hunter stopped in at an isolated bar in the interior of Africa. As he lounged at the bar downing a strong native brew, in walked a tiny man about one foot high immaculately dressed in a British Army uniform.

Noticing the tourist staring open-mouthed at the diminutive newcomer, the bartender remarked, "Apparently you haven't met the Major before. Speak up, Major—tell the Yank about the time you called the witch doctor a bloody fake."

14

"Madame," said the psychiatrist, "you haven't got a complex; you *are* inferior."

"Why does your grandmother read the Bible so much?"

"I think she's cramming for her finals."

"Horace, dear," she said softly, "can you drive with one hand?"

"Yes, my sweet"

"Then you better wipe your nose. It's running."

"Waiter, there is a fly in my soup."

"That's very possible; the chef used to be a tailor."

Notice on the bulletin board of the zoology department:

"We don't begrudge your taking a little alcohol, but please return our specimens."

Little Sheldon seemed to be enjoying himself thoroughly at the zoo with his father. As they were looking at the lions, however, a troubled look came over the boy's face and his father asked him what was the matter.

"I was just wondering, Daddy. In case a lion breaks loose and eats you, what number bus do I take home?"

"Mother, come here quickly!"

"What's the matter, dear?"

"Billy just ate the raisins off that sticky brown paper!"

17

18

A man was studying the menu at a roadside restaurant.

"What's the difference between the blue-plate special and the white-plate special?" he asked the waiter.

"The white-plate special is ten cents extra," explained the waiter.

"Is the food any better?"

"No, but we wash the plates."

Mother: "Do you like your new nurse, Sheldon?"
Sheldon: "No, I hate her. I'd like to grab her and bite her neck like Daddy does."

"I had an operation and the doc left a sponge in me."

"Got any pain?"

"No. But, boy, do I get thirsty!"

A small boy walked into a drug store and asked the clerk for some talcum powder.

"Certainly, Sonny," said the druggist. "Just walk this way please."

"If I could walk that way," the boy said, "I wouldn't need the talcum."

Whistler, the famous painter, was exasperated when he came home from work one night and found his mother sitting in the middle of the living room floor.

"What's the matter, Ma?" he demanded. "You off your rocker?"

20

"Why, no, Mrs. Sontag, I haven't seen him all day."

Patient: "Give it to me straight, Doc—how am I?"
Doctor: "Well, if you feel as bad as you look, you've come too late."

"I'm a little girl."
"I'm a little boy."
"How do you know you're a little boy?"
"Wait till the nurse goes out and I'll show you."
When the nurse left, the baby pulled up his dress.
"See? Blue booties."

"I don't DIG, man."

There was a neurotic from Natchez
Who wrote in weird Freudian scratches.
Her Doc was impressed,
Till she finally confessed
That she wrote with her toes and burnt matches.

A farmer once called his cow Zephyr;
She seemed such an amiable hephyr.
When the farmer drew near,
She kicked off his ear,
Which made him considerably dephyr.

Then there was the case of the cow that went dry—udder failure.

Drunk: "Aw lemme alone. Nobody cares if I drink myself to death."
Host: "I do. You're using my liquor."

Kindergarten Teacher: "Let's all draw with our crayons what we'd like to be when we grow up."

At the end of thirty minutes every child handed in a paper except little Sheldon.

"Why, Sheldon," his teacher said, "isn't there anything you want to be when you grow up?"

"Sure, teacher," replied Sheldon, "I want to be married, but I don't know how to draw it."

24

"He wants a room with hot and cold running blood."

"Eustace!" called Mama, "are you spitting into that fish bowl?"

"No, Ma, but I'm coming closer with every one."

Teacher: "Now, children, if I saw a man beating a donkey and stopped him, what virtue would I be showing?"

Sheldon: "Brotherly love."

A forest ranger in New Mexico frequently saw an Indian riding his horse up the canyon trail, his squaw trudging along behind him.

"Why is it," the ranger asked one day, "that you always ride and your wife walks?"

"Because," was the solemn reply, "she no gottum horse."

The old lady bent over the carriage: "Oooo, you sweet little thing. I could eat you."

"The hell you could. You haven't got any teeth."

Hollywood Story: The wife rushed into her house screaming to her actor husband, "Darling, come quick. Your kids and my kids are beating up our kids!"

27

hal higdon

School was out and little Julius came bursting into the house crying bitterly.

"The kids beat me up, Mommy. They said I have a big head."

"Now, Julius, don't you listen to them," soothed his mother. "It's not true you have a big head."

So, partly convinced, Julius returned to school the next day. That afternoon the scene was repeated, and again his mother repeated her words of reassurance.

"So now calm down," she said, "because I would like you to run down to the store and get me nine pounds of potatoes."

"Okay, Mom. Gimme a bag to put them in," replied Julius.

"A bag! What do you need a bag for?" asked his mother. "Carry them in your cap."

29

*"Who in Hell
do you want?"*

Elsie the cow was on one side of the fence and Ferdinand the bull was on the other side. Elsie gave Ferdinand a wink and he leaped over the fence to her side.

"Aren't you Ferdinand the bull?" she asked.

"Just call me Ferdinand; the fence was higher than I thought."

"Your new little brother has just arrived, Sheldon."

"Where'd he come from, Daddy?"

"From a far-away country."

"Another damned alien."

Teacher: "George Washington not only chopped down his father's cherry tree, but he also admitted doing it. Now do you know why his father didn't punish him?"

Sheldon: "Because George still had the axe in his hand."

"How come your father's so mad about us using his car last night?"

"That was him we ran down."

The young father was explaining that he had found a sure-fire method for putting the baby to sleep.

"I toss it up in the air again and again."

"How does that put it to sleep?" asked his neighbor.

"We have very low ceilings."

31

"Awright, Ella, awright . . . I know your mother told you to be in by midnight, but heck, a few minutes won't . . ."

"I guess I've lost another pupil," said the professor as his glass eye rolled down the sink.

Chaplain (to condemned man in electric chair): "Can I do anything for you?"
Prisoner: "Yeah. Hold my hand."

District Attorney: "Now tell the jury the truth please. Why did you shoot your husband with a bow and arrow?"
Defendant: "I didn't want to wake the children."

"Warmer ... warmer ..."

The nudists were having a costume party and one of the ladies was worrying about what to wear.

"Well," drawled one, "with my varicose veins I think I'll go as a road map."

I got a dog, his name is Rover.
He's fluffy and soft and brown all over.
He's as cute and cuddly as sugar babies.
It's sure too bad that he's got rabies.

Hollywood scene; two children are talking:
"I've got two brothers and sisters. How many do you have?"

"I don't have any, but I've got three papas by my first mama, and four mamas by my first papa."

34

A big-time gambler had just died. The funeral drew a heavy crowd, mainly his professional friends. In eulogy, the speaker said, "Nick is not dead. He only sleeps."

From the rear came a voice, "I've got a couple grand that says he don't wake up."

Cannibal Chief (to victim): "What did you do for a living?"
Victim: "I was an associate editor."
Chief: "Cheer up. After tonight you'll be editor-in-chief."

Definition of an Ivy League kiss: A belt in the mouth.

36

"You killed him, you cook him!"

There was a knock on the door. Mrs. Miffin opened it.

"Are you the Widow Miffin?" a small boy asked.

"I'm Mrs. Miffin," she replied, "but I'm not a widow."

"Oh, no?" replied the little boy, "wait till you see what they're carrying upstairs."

39

The cannibal entered the dining room aboard the luxury ocean liner.

"Would you care for a menu?" the steward asked.

"No, just bring me the passenger list."

"How old are you?" asked the funeral director.

"Ninety-seven."

"Hardly worth going home, is it?"

Sweet Little Girl: "Mommy, mommy, the boy next door broke my dolly."

Mommy: "Why, that's terrible, dear. How did he do it?"

Little Girl: "I hit him over the head with it."

"Grandmother! Use the bottle opener—you'll ruin your gums."

40

The Romans gave up their big holidays because of the terrific overhead. The lions ate up all their prophets.

First Toddler: "Your daddy can't hold a candle to what my daddy can do."
Second Toddler: "What does your daddy do?"
First Toddler: "Makes gun powder."

The fourth grader was in bed with a cold and a high temperature.
"How high is it, Doctor?" he wanted to know.
"A hundred and three, son," said the doctor.
"What's the world's record?"

Little Tot: "Mommy, can we go to a movie?"
Mommy: "If it isn't a gangster movie."
Tot: "It's not. It's 'The Dwarf Rats Meet the Four-legged Zombie Monsters.'"
Mom: "All right, dear. Just so it isn't about gangsters."

Then there was the principal who had to dismiss the cross-eyed teacher because she had no control over her pupils.

"He fell in, came up, murmured 'Mmm, mmm, good,'
and sank."

Little Bobbie tripped and fell on his face on the sidewalk. An elderly lady rushed over to help him to his feet.

"Now, little boy, you must be brave about this," she purred. "You mustn't cry."

"Cry, my foot," replied Bobbie, "I'm going to sue hell out of somebody."

"You knew very well the train would run over little Homer when you put him on the tracks."

"I gave him a time-table, didn't I?"

"Do you realize, George, that this room we rented is supposed to be haunted by a ghost that returns every year on this date at midnight to find a human sacrifice? . . . George? George!"

43

"You left a dirty ring in the tub."

"I have a rather irregular request from that man in the dark cape," the blood bank attendant told his superior.

"What's that?" asked the boss.

"Well, sir," the attendant explained, "he wants two pints to take out."

The meanest man in the world is the warden who put a tack on the electric chair.

He had been bitten by a dog, but didn't give it much thought until he noticed that the wound was taking a remarkably long time to heal. Finally he consulted a doctor, who took one look at the wound and ordered the dog brought in.

Just as the doctor suspected, the dog had rabies. Since it was too late to give the patient a serum, the doctor felt he had to prepare him for the worst.

The poor man sat down at the doctor's desk and began to write. The physician tried to comfort him.

"Perhaps it won't be so bad," he said. "You needn't make out your will right now."

"I'm not making out any will," replied the man. "I'm just writing out a list of people I'm going to bite."

The weird scientist looked over reports on his life-preserving tonic.

"Hmmm," he mused, "I see where my elixir has had its first failure—a ninety-eight-year-old woman. Ahhhh, but what's this? They saved the baby."

45

46

He was so sick that his doctor ordered him to take a long rest cure in Florida. But after two months he died anyway.

Shipped back home, the corpse was viewed by the widow and her brother. "Herman," she sighed, "he does look nice, doesn't he?"

"He sure does," replied Herman. "Who wouldn't after two months in Florida?"

"They had to shoot poor Fido last week."
"Was he mad?"
"He wasn't any too pleased."

"I don't care what you're inventing, Mr. Whitney, keep your cotton-pickin' hands off my gin!"

"Well," said the missionary to his colleague, speaking from inside the cannibal's pot, "at least this will be their first taste of religion."

Little Girl Cannibal: "Mommy, is that airplane up there good to eat?"

Mamma Cannibal: "Just like a lobster, dear. Only what's inside."

The firing squad was escorting a prisoner to his place of execution. It was a dismal march in a pouring rain.

"What a terrible morning to die," muttered the condemned man.

"What are you kicking about?" asked the guard. "We gotta march back in it."

SIGALE

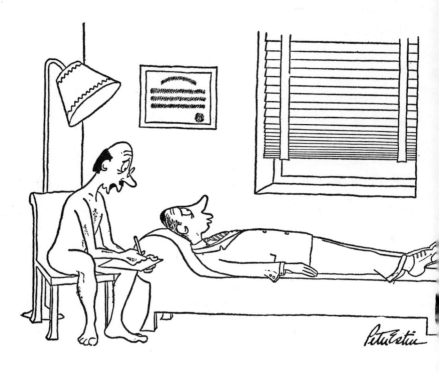

"Your trouble, Mr. Olson, is you're inhibited."

The judge arraigned the little boy in court.

"You mean to tell me, young man," the judge said in disbelief, "that you shot your grandmother for 25 cents?"

"You know how it is, Judge," the culprit replied, "two bits here, two bits there . . . it adds up."

Little Willie shot his sister;
She was dead before we missed her.
Willie's always up to tricks.
Ain't he cute? He's only six.

He was sitting on the curb with a cigarette in one hand and the neck of a flask protruding from his hip pocket.

An old lady came up to him and said, "Sonny, why aren't you in school?"

"Lady, I'm only three."

49

The little boy refused to eat. In desperation, his frantic mother took him to a psychiatrist who tried to tempt the lad with all manner of goodies. Nothing worked. Finally the doc threw up his hands and said, "All right, what would *you* like to eat?"

"Worms," replied the boy.

Not to be outsmarted, the doctor sent his nurse out for a plate of them. "Here," he shouted at the boy.

"I want them fried," the youngster wailed.

Again the nurse was sent out and returned with a heaping plate of fried worms.

"I only want one," yelled the boy.

The doctor promptly got rid of all but one. "Now," he bellowed, "eat!"

"You eat half!" insisted the boy.

The doctor gagged the fried worm down, then dangled the remaining portion in the little tyke's face. The boy shook with tears.

"Now what's the matter?" growled the exasperated doctor.

"You ate my half!"

51

Soon after the newlyweds came back from their honeymoon, the bride cooked her first chicken. When the husband began to carve it, he asked, "What did you stuff it with, dear?"

"I didn't have to stuff it," she replied. "It wasn't hollow."

"Yes, Jones, it's true that your wife is at death's door. But I think we can pull her through."

"I don't care if your name *is* Tom Dooley, get the hell out of my oak tree!"

Then there was the vampire actress who was waiting for a character she could really sink her teeth into.

"Mommy, I fell into the well and almost drowned."
"So wipe your feet before you come in the house."

The village idiot, who had never seen a parrot, one day noticed one perched atop a farmhouse gable. Attracted by the bright plumage, he ran to fetch a ladder, climbed on the roof, and was about to clap his cap over the bird when the parrot fixed him with a beady eye and asked, "What the hell do you think *you're* doing?"
"Gosh, I didn't mean nothin'," said the idiot, "I thought you was a bird."

53

54

"I don't care if your name *is* Napoleon, get your hand out of my blouse!"

Then there was the nine-year-old who shot both his parents and pled with the judge for mercy because he was an orphan.

The Miami playgirl was sinking fast and she knew it. With her doctor and loved ones around, she spoke with great effort:
"Farewell, farewell, I'm dying, cha-cha-cha."

"Mommy, are you *sure* this is the way to make pizza?"
"Shut up and get back in the oven!"

"Tired? Nervous? Fidgety? Have that 'run-down' feeling all the time? Act now! Don't wait a second! Write to the New York Amalgamated Casket and Mausoleum Co. for your free booklet. . . ."

"Good test for your abdominal muscles," read an advertisement. "Grab your feet. Put them together on the floor. Now bend to the right at the waist and sit down to the left of your feet. Lift yourself up with your abdominal muscles. Now bend to the left at the waist and sit down to the right of your feet. Keep it up and let us know the result."

Read the first letter: "Hernia."

"Best neck I've had in years. . . ."

57

"Shirley, is there something wrong with you? You seem smaller than when I saw you last year."

"That's right. I'm shrinking. My doctor says I'm an atavistic throwback."

"So what else is new?"

"Daddy, Mommy kissed the iceman this morning."

"Why is she wasting time with *him?* We owe the grocer $20."

Then there was the butcher who backed into the meat grinder and got a little behind in his orders.

"I don't care what your reason is, Mrs. Lincoln, I still say no ticket refunds."

"How many hearts have you broken with that great big beautiful eye. . . ."

A man who bred prize bulldogs was walking his grand champion down the street. Suddenly another man appeared walking a strange, yellowish animal, the oddest-looking dog you've ever seen.

Their owners came abreast, the dogs began to growl at one another, and with a vicious swipe, the yellow bit the prize bulldog's head off.

Infuriated, the champion's owner demanded, "What kind of a dog do you call that?"

"Well, sir," replied the owner, "before I cut his tail off and painted him yellow, folks called him an alligator."

Mother: "Well, children, what have you been doing while I've been out shopping?"

Children: "Oh, Mommy, we've been having so much fun! We've got Granny's hearing aid up to 50,000 watts—and you should see her nose glow!"

"I don't care what you're president of, get your hands off my golf club!"

"I think the green one is the stronger swimmer."

"What are we having for supper. Mother?"

"Hey, are we really juvenile delinquents?"
"Don't bother me. I'm stropping my razor."

"Are you still engaged to that girl with the wooden leg?"
"No. I got mad at her and broke it off."

"Damn dog died."

61

"Mommy, is Sheldon stuck-up?"
"No, dear, I don't think so."
"Then why won't he come out of that old ice-box?"

Little Bertha insisted that she be permitted to serve the tea when her mother was entertaining her club. Her mother consented. However, she became annoyed by the long delay, and asked, "Why were you so long, my dear?"

"I couldn't find the tea strainer," said Bertha.

"Then how did you strain it so well?"

"I used the fly-swatter."

"Why is Daddy running so fast?"
"Shut up, dear, and keep shooting."

Then there was the enterprising man seen at the crematorium gathering up ashes—which he sends to cannibals so they can have instant people.

Little Boy: "Mommy, sing me a lullaby."
Mommy: "Hold my beer for me, angel, and I'll see if I can get one on the radio."

"Lady," said the little boy, "if you give us a quarter, my little brother will imitate a hen."

"What will he do," asked the lady, "cackle?"

"No," answered the little boy in disgust. "He wouldn't do a cheap imitation like that; he'll eat a worm."

"Ladyfinger?"

STILL MORE
Sick Jokes
& EVEN GRIMMER CARTOONS

ACKNOWLEDGMENTS

The editor wishes to thank the following publications for cartoons used in this book:

Stanford CHAPARRAL *(Pages 19, 25, 57)*
University of Washington COLUMNS *(Pages 9, 41, 61)*
Southern Illinois University KING TUT *(Page 39)*
Harvard LAMPOON *(Pages 13, 21, 31, 55)*
San Jose LYKE *(Page 27)*
University of Florida ORANGE PEEL *(Pages 45, 51)*
University of California PELICAN *(Page 23)*
Texas RANGER *(Pages 11, 15, 17, 47)*
University of Missouri SHOWME *(Page 33)*
M.I.T. VooDoo *(Page 37)*
Cornell WIDOW *(Page 29)*

"Don't you think, Doctor, you've overcharged for attending Jimmy when he had the measles?"

"You must remember, Mrs. Brown, that the bill covers twenty-three visits."

"Yes, but you forget that he infected the whole school."

"He lost both legs in a train wreck last year."
"Did the railroad treat him right?"
"He can't kick."

"I had two punctures in one day."
"How did that happen?"
"I ran over a man with a wing collar."

10

Death is just Nature's way of telling you to slow down.

"Your father just fell into the fireplace."
"Well, poke him up. It's chilly in here."

And then there was the juvenile delinquent who was very careful about his health. He smoked only filter-tipped marijuanas.

"I say, chap, your wife has fallen into the well."
"Oh, that's all right. We use city water now."

"... hope you won't think I'm a coward for saying this but I had a good scare last week. As a rule nothing bothers me, mind you, but you see we were traversing this. . ."

"I'm wondering—"

"About what?"

"About a fellow I know. He was in an accident and lost both hands."

"Well, what are you wondering about?"

"I wonder how he feels."

And then there was the girl who was so cross-eyed that when she cried, the tears from her right eye fell on her left cheek.

One day in the jungle an explorer came upon some cannibals who were just about to eat a meal. The head of the tribe confided to the white man that he had been educated in Britain and had been to Oxford.

"Do you mean to say," asked the amazed explorer, "that you went to a university and yet you still eat your enemies?"

"Oh yes," was the reply. "But of course I now use a knife and fork."

12

"*But mine's a hydrogen bomb!*"

"Sheldon, why did you kick your little sister in the stomach?"

"Couldn't help it. She turned around too quick."

"I just saw a girl with a glass eye."

"How do you know? Did she tell you?"

"No, stupid. It came out in the conversation."

"Are my seams straight?"

"Your seams are okay. It's your legs that are twisted."

"All this talk about back-seat drivers is overrated. I've been driving for twenty years and I've never heard a word from behind."

"What sort of car do you drive?"

"A hearse."

"You rang, sir?"

16

"How do you know your father's dead?"
"He doesn't move when I kick him."

"Ma, I just put a stick of dynamite under teacher's chair."
"Why that's terrible, Sheldon. You march yourself right back to school immediately."
"What school?"

"Hey, Ma, Sheldon's on fire!"
"Well, shut off the furnace. There's no use wasting coal."

And then there was the judge who told the condemned man, "You'll die when you hear this one."

"You drove one of your passengers to a secluded spot, strangled him, and dismembered his body. What have you to say?"

"Who's going to pay the cab fare?"

"Now I'm taller than she is," said the husband gleefully.

"Have you gotten elevator shoes?"

"No, she just had her legs amputated."

The inmates of a mental institution were listening to modern jazz records. One patient at last could contain himself no longer. He jumped up and started banging his head against the wall in tune to the music. The other inmates applauded and shouted, "Sane, man, sane!"

"Your fortune: You now have Asiatic flu."

20

"When I die, I want to be cremated," the man said.
"That would be just like you," replied his wife, "to go away and leave ashes lying all over the house."

"Do you have rat poison?"
"Yes, shall I wrap it."
"No, I'll have it here."

The newspapers report a current hate-campaign: they go around putting Rx signs on Christian Science reading rooms.

"I saw the first robin today."
"In December?"
"Yeah. Frozen to the ground."

"I think it's Beechnut!"

Mr. and Mrs. Bird were building a nest in the trees.

Suddenly Mrs. Bird noticed there was a large hole in the bottom of the nest. Turning to Mr. Bird, she asked why.

"Well," said Mr. Bird, "because I adore marriage, but I just hate children."

The hearse rounded the corner at sixty miles an hour.

Suddenly the back door opened up and the casket slid out, banged into the curb and landed on the sidewalk at the feet of a beatnik.

Spreading out his arms he yelled, "Safe!"

He couldn't decide on a costume for the party. Finally he had an inspiration.

Spraying deodorant over his beard, he showed up as an armpit.

"I don't agree with everything Mather does either, but at least he's anti-devil."

24

The woman's husband was laid out in the funeral parlor.

Suddenly she decided she didn't like the brown suit her husband had on.

Walking up to the funeral director, she said, "I see another man wearing a blue suit in the next parlor. Blue was my husband's favorite color and I'd like him laid out in a blue suit."

The funeral director was happy to comply, and told the woman to return in an hour and the change would be made.

When the hour was up, the woman returned and happily found her husband now lying in a blue suit, the other one in a brown one.

"However did you change suits?" she asked the undertaker.

"I didn't change suits," he replied, "I found it was easier just to switch heads."

"Hang on, Joe, we'll get you out."

The cats were barreling along the highway in their souped-up car at eighty miles an hour.

Suddenly the door flew open.

Said one cat to the other, "Like who got out, man?"

"Now look me right in the face."

"Doctor, I got my own problems."

A traveling salesman's car broke down. After walking for several hours, he spotted a mountaineer's shack.

He knocked at the door and a bearded man with a shotgun appeared.

"My car has stalled, sir, and I wonder if I could stay the night?" he asked, chuckling inwardly as he waited the inevitable answer.

"Wal," drawled the mountaineer, "you could sleep with my daughter but she's in an iron lung."

"Do you ever get the feeling you've been mistreated?"

28

He was lying in a pool of blood when two of his friends came along.

"What should I do, man?" he pleaded.

"Fingerpaint, man, fingerpaint."

A man just got a car for his wife. Now, that's what you call Fair Trade.

The woman was watching a production of *My Fair Lady*.

Suddenly a man approached her and asked, "Pardon me, Madam, but do you mind if I occupy that empty seat next to you?"

"Not at all," she replied. "I expected it to be taken when I bought the tickets, but all my friends are at my husband's funeral."

The beatnik stood in the head of the Statue of Liberty.

Disappointed with the view he climbed out to the ear and hung by it.

A police helicopter flew by and the officer shouted, "Hey, what are you supposed to be doing?"

Replied the beatnik, "Like, man, I'm an earring!"

HE: "Whisper those three little words that will make me walk on air."

SHE: "Go hang yourself."

"May, it shore is too bad about our two daughters laying up thar in that cemetery."

"Shore is, Paw. Sometimes I wish they wuz dead!"

32

"The editor hanged himself a few minutes ago."
"Have they cut him down?"
"Not yet. He isn't dead."

> *Beneath this stone lies Murphy.*
> *They buried him today.*
> *He lived the life of Riley,*
> *While Riley was away.*

The drunk was telling of his ways as a salesman.

"Yesh," he said, "I sold a bottle of my miracle rub to a cripple. He rubbed some on his right leg and threw away his right crutch. Then he rubbed some on left leg and threw away his left crutch."

"Well, what happened then?" asked his listener.

"Hell, he fell flat on his face. He couldn't walk without his crutches."

"It's nothing, officer, I'm cooking the baby."

The patient with high blood pressure was worried. "Tell me, Doc," he asked, "Just how sick am I?"

"Let me put it this way," said the doctor, "If it wasn't for your skin, you'd be a fountain."

Ruth rode on my motor-bike,
Directly back of me;
I hit a bump at sixty-five,
And rode on ruthlessly.

Two cannibals met in a mental institution. One was tearing out pictures of men, women, and children from a magazine, stuffing them into his mouth and eating them.

"Tell me," said the other, "is that dehydrated stuff really that good?"

34

"What happened to your hand, kid?"
"I sawed the top of my finger off."
"Dear, dear, how did you do that?"
"Sawing."

A faith healer ran into his old friend Max and asked him how things were going.

"Not so good," was the pained reply. "My brother is very sick."

"Your brother isn't sick," contradicted the faith healer, "he only thinks he's sick. Remember that, he only thinks he's sick."

Two months later they met again and the faith healer asked Max:

"How's your brother now."

"Worse," groaned Max, "he thinks he's dead."

36

A man approached a little boy sitting on a street corner.

"I-I-I-I s-s-say, little b-b-b-boy, c-c-ould you direct me t-t-t-to the fire station?"

The little boy looked up at him and said nothing but slowly shook his head.

"L-L-L-Look here, are you s-s-s-sure you c-c-c-can't direct m-m-me to the fire station?"

The boy looked up again and slowly nodded his head.

"W-W-W-Well thank y-y-y-you anyway," said the man, and strode off.

At this another man who had witnessed the whole affair walked up and glared at the youth.

"Boy," he said, "why didn't you tell that man where the fire department was? You've been living in this town a long time, haven't you?"

"Yeah," answered the boy, "b-b-b-but do y-y-y-you think I w-w-wanna get the h-h-h-h-hell s-s-s-slapped out of m-m-m-me?"

Then there was the deaf mute who said so many dirty words that his mother had to wash his hands.

"Who's that close-mouthed fellow over there?"

"He ain't close-mouthed. He's just waiting for the janitor to come back with the spittoon."

"The college is on fire!" shouted a passing motorist to a sophomore one Saturday morning.

"I know it," said the sophomore.

"Then why aren't you doing something about it?" cried the motorist.

"Oh, I am!" replied the sophomore, "Ever since it started I've been praying for rain.

40

A beautiful blonde walked into a Chicago police station and gave the desk sergeant a detailed description of a man who had dragged her by the hair down three flights of stairs, threatened to choke her to death and finally beat her up.

"With that description, we'll have him arrested and put in jail in practically no time," said the desk sergeant. "But I don't want him arrested," the young woman protested. "Just find him for me. He promised to marry me."

WILL: "She treated me badly."
BILL: "She treated me worse."
WILL: "Impossible! She jilted me."
BILL: "She married me."

My wife and I sure had a good time at the beach last summer. First she'd bury me in the sand, then I'd bury her. This summer I'm going back and dig her up.

"He likes children."

"Why the black shroud on your roomie's bed?"
"Black shroud, hell! That's his sheet!"

First Cannibal: "Am I late for dinner?"
Second Cannibal: "Yes, everybody's eaten."

The tramp was sitting with his back to a hedge by the wayside, munching at some scraps wrapped in a newspaper. A lady, out walking with her pet Pomeranian, strolled past. The little dog ran to the tramp and tried to muzzle the food. The tramp smiled expansively on the lady. "Shall I throw the little dog a bit, mum?" he asked.

The lady smiled a gracious assent, and the tramp caught the dog by the nape of the neck and tossed it over the hedge.

Farmer Thomas' barn had just gone up in smoke, and his insurance agent was trying to explain that he couldn't collect cash for it.

"Read the policy," he insisted. "All our company can do is build you another barn exactly like the one that's been destroyed."

Farmer Thomas, apoplectic with rage, thundered, "If that's the way you varmints do business, cancel the policy on my wife before it's too late."

The Sunday gospel-shouter was in great form. "Everything God made is perfect," he preached.

A hunchback rose from the rear of the auditorium. "What about me?"

"Why," said the preacher, "you're the most perfect hunchback I ever saw!"

44

"Sheldon, the baby has swallowed the matches!"
"Here, use my lighter."

A diamond-bedecked movie star, last to leave the theatre after a gala film premiere, was heading up the aisle when she noticed one of the cleaning women staring after her. Suddenly, a cry of "Mother" filled the empty theatre and the two women rushed together in an embrace.

When, minutes later, the star, dabbing her eyes, finally tore loose and disappeared into her waiting Rolls-Royce, the cleaning woman proudly turned to her fellow workers. "You got to admit it," she smiled, "Ma sure is a good-lookin' woman."

"Oh yeah? How would you like your daughter married to one?"

Seems George was playing his usual eighteen holes one Saturday afternoon. Teeing off from the 17th hole, he sliced into the rough over near the edge of the fairway. Just as he was about to chip out, he noticed a long funeral procession going past on a nearby street. Reverently, George removed his hat and stood at attention until the procession had passed. Then he continued his game, finishing with a birdie on the eighteenth. Later, at the clubhouse, a fellow golfer greeted George. "Say, that was a nice gesture you made today, George."

"What do you mean?" asked George.

"I mean it was nice of you to take off your cap and stand respectfully when that funeral went by," the friend replied.

"Oh yes," said George. "We would have been married thirty years next month."

46

"Once there was a nice man who loved his little daughter very much. . ."

48

Distressed Young Mother (traveling with crying infant): Dear me, I just don't know what to do with this child.

Bachelor (in next seat): Shall I open the window for you?

A rich bachelor girl made it a practice to invite several servicemen each weekend to her sumptuous country estate. One week a good-looking officer showed up alone. It was a case of love at first sight. The impact was terrific. As he was leaving, he held her in a close embrace. Kissing her, he asked: "Suppose dear, after a few months you should find that something was, er, wrong—what would you do?"

"Why—why—I would shoot myself!"

He patted her on the back encouragingly. "Atta girl!"

"I shore wish I had my wife back," sighed the man from the Ozarks.

"Where is she?" asked a friend.

"Sold her for a jug of mountain dew."

"I reckon you're beginning to miss her."

"Nope. I'm thirsty again."

Women's hair, beautiful hair,
What words of praise I utter,
But, oh, how sick it makes me feel
To find it in the butter.

"Did you ever have this before?"

"Yes, Doctor."

"Well, you've got it again."

And then there's this new deodorant called "Vanish" which makes you invisible and everybody wonders where the odor is coming from.

"This poor fellow," explained the doctor to the people touring through the asylum, "has a very sad history. See how he fondles that large doll. He spends most of his time like that. He was engaged to a girl whom he loved very deeply. She jilted him, however, and married another man, while this one lost his reason over the affair."

They passed along the corridor to the next cell, which was barred and thickly padded.

"And this," resumed the doctor, "is the other man."

"We have to let him play—it's his bat."

52

"I finally stopped my roommate from biting his nails."

"How?"

"I made him wear shoes."

"Hey!" cried Satan to the new arrival. "You act as if you owned the place!"

"I do," came the reply. "My wife gave it to me before I died!"

Q. "When is the only time a woman is justified in spitting in a man's face?"

A. "When his mustache is on fire."

It happened aboard a trans-Atlantic liner.

A steward was walking along the promenade deck with a large bowl of soup when the ship rolled exceptionally hard and he dumped the entire bowl onto the shirt front of a passenger sleeping in a deck chair.

Thinking fast, the steward awoke the man and said, consolingly, "I do hope you're feeling better now, sir."

Want ad: Man to work as garbage collector. $50 a week and all you can eat.

Teacher: "Johnny, do you wish to leave the room?"
Johnny: "I ain't hitch-hiking."

"I'm anxious to make this shot. That's my mother-in-law up on the clubhouse porch."

"Don't be a fool, you can't hit her at 200 yards."

No wonder the undertaker was doing a fantastic business. He had a good location—right near the doctor's office.

"Mommy, Mommy, Johnny threw up."

"Then why are you crying, Gladys?"

"Because he's getting all the big pieces."

She was reading about birth and death statistics.

Suddenly she turned to a man near her and said, "Do you know that every time I breathe a man dies?"

"Very interesting," he returned. "Have you tried toothpaste?"

56

"Excuse me, Mrs. Jones, my daughter has lost her arrow."

"Where is it?"

"I think it's stuck in your son."

The gentleman was on his way home when he passed a house and saw through the window a woman hitting a small boy over the head with a loaf of bread.

Next day he passed, and the next, and the next, and each time the woman was hitting the boy on the head with a loaf of bread.

Finally one Tuesday when he passed, he saw her hitting the boy on the head with a cake.

"Hello," he said putting his head in through the window, "run out of bread today?"

"Of course not," replied the woman, "it's his birthday."

58

A purchasing agent became ill and called in a specialist.

The specialist, as he stood by the bedside, said, "Yes, I can cure you."

"What will it cost?" asked the purchasing agent faintly.

"Five hundred dollars."

"You'll have to shave your price a little," replied the purchasing agent. "I have a better bid from the undertaker."

The bandage-covered patient who lay in the hospital bed spoke dazedly to his visiting pal:

"Wh-what happened?"

"You absorbed one too many last night, and then you made a bet that you could jump out of the window and fly around the block."

"Why," screamed the beat-up human, "didn't you stop me?"

"Stop you, hell—I had $25 on you."

If it weren't for Edison, we'd all be watching TV by candlelight.

Two psychiatrists passed each other on the street. "You're fine," said one. "How am I?"

"For leprosy, go to Devil's Island."
"Is that good for it, Doctor?"
"That's where I got mine."

Friend (at a funeral): "It must be hard to lose a wife."
Bereaved: "Almost impossible."

Mangled Pedestrian: "What's the matter, are you blind?"
Motorist: "Blind?—I hit ya didn't I?"

"Are you sure I'll recover?" an anxious patient asked his doctor. "I've heard that doctors sometimes give wrong diagnoses and treat patients for pneumonia who later die of typhoid fever."

"Don't worry," replied the doctor, "if I treat a man for pneumonia, he dies of pneumonia."

"I made a killing in the market today."
"Really?"
"Yeah. I shot the manager of the A & P."

"I still can't believe you don't have a navel."
"Well, Doctor, I'm afraid it's true."
"It's the most complete rejection of mother I've ever seen."

"Get your damn foot off my chair!"

"Sure it was a nice holiday, but who wants to clean up after all those reindeer?"

"My husband is an angel."
"You mean he finally reformed?"
"No, he went looking for a gas leak with a match."

"You must help me, doctor," said the patient to his psychiatrist. "I can't remember anything for more than a few minutes. It's driving me crazy."

"How long has this been going on?" asked the psychiatrist gently.

"How long has what been going on?" replied the man.